Here I Am...

A memoir for motivational purposes

Entity

S.H.E. PUBLISHING, LLC

For information contact:
info@shepublishingllc.com or visit www.shepublishingllc.com

Cover and Title Page Design by Nabin

Library of Congress Control Number: 2024946774
ISBN: 978-1-964061-19-1 (*paperback*)
First Edition: October 2024
10 9 8 7 6 5 4 3 2 1

NaNa, Granpi, PawPaw, 414.... I did it.

I Love You.

Foreword

"Wings of Destiny"...

When I met Entity two decades ago supporting the 101st Combat Aviation Brigade, our motto may as well have been written for her. Some people's life stories give away the ending in the first chapter. Others might be a comforting coffeehouse read, have a twist ending or ramble endlessly without a clear direction.

With Entity, there's always been an underlying saga of determination in the face of life's complexity. She's always known exactly where she was going, no matter what interfered. Her life is an allegory of the importance of relationships; knowing and living your values; seeking a meaningful, purposeful existence even when life's challenges make it a seemingly insurmountable task. We don't always get to choose our experiences in life, but as part of my own "chosen family", Entity's story powerfully shows how we continually shape and refine ourselves, how we survive and thrive.

G. W. B. , Chief Warrant Officer 5, U.S. Army., 2024.

Contents

See it's ugly sometimes...

That's if it's even clear enough for me to see...

All the dirt and smudges in the way....

I just want to wipe it away....

Sometimes it'll clean one part, but only make the rest worse....

I hear you; you see beauty through it all....

Your angle is different....

Outside looking in....

I'll know that version one day too....

She seems cool....

Just out of reach....

I'll push through though....

I'll get to know her....

I mean what's life....

What's success....

If you don't know the main character....

How I see the view....

It's different....

Self.

It's funny really, how you look back at your life at times, and everything and nothing makes sense. I can remember as I lived my life over the years, always feeling like I was watching a movie, or acting out a story that was already written. The way you're raised gives you a blueprint of sorts, whether it's good or bad. It can show you everything that you should be, or everything and everyone that you want to avoid.

Little girl...

Brown skin...

White Dress...

Big Bows....

Lace socks....

Patent Leather Shoes....

I was you....

Sitting on the porch at my NaNa's house, watching people, cars, inner city life; the "hood", it didn't scare me, because it was home. There was comfort in it all. Nana's house was paradise in the middle of it all. My first memories, right there. I always knew I was supposed to step off that porch, even then. Little, unscarred, Vaseline covered, burnt sienna crayon brown colored legs, swinging. NaNa would tell me I better not leave that porch, but to sit right there.

I had to get up.
I was meant to.
I had to.

It's my belief that we all know early on, who and what we are. We have a feeling deep down, it pulls us. Some of us listen to those voices that whisper loudly within. Some of us, well, we fear ourselves. See there's never really anything in your way. Obstacles are only in the way, if you don't figure out how to get around them.

I thank my family, for showing me the beauty in my environment, shading my eyes from the ugly parts when possible. As soon as I stepped off that porch on my own, I realized that everything wasn't always beautiful. There was beauty in all things, but that didn't make it beautiful. There was drugs, violence, neglect, pimps & hoes, abuse, exploitation, gangs, failure, sex (both consensual and non consensual), and all kinds of other shit in the way. I could go into detail about it all, but I'm not. You'll hear parts of what matters most along the way. For what it's worth, it made me. Milwaukee, Wisconsin, the Northside, it made me.

I say all of this, to say that we all come from something. That place, those things, they made you. Even the ugliest parts of your story, they made you. So many people are ashamed of the blemishes and scars in their life's story, don't be. Those things, those moments, they are the parts of you that you should be proud of. In spite of what happened, what was done, what mistake was made, what you could or couldn't control, you made it. You are now on the other side of it all. There's strength in that alone.

Society has told us that being strong is regular, everyday shit; well, I'm here to say that it's not. If that was the case, if everyone was strong, if everyone was able to overcome and succeed, I wouldn't be writing this. This book is for everyone who needs to know or remember who they are, and what they're capable of. This is for those that need a reminder to be proud of how far they've come.

I am volunteering myself and parts of my story, so that someone who truly needs it, can see that imperfections are necessary too. No matter how perfect things may look from the outside, we are all battling something, we were all hurt by someone, and vice versa.

Never let your environment, your story, define you; it's just a part of it all. You keep going, keep growing, keep living and you'll find that there's always more to come. I know that in that moment, it may not seem that way....

That little girl on her NaNa's porch, she grew. She became that awkward girl with the big glasses, small frame, big dreams, but no idea how. She didn't fit in, in those middle years. She didn't try too hard though, she was just 'her'. Sometimes being 'her' worked, sometimes it didn't, but she was still her.

That awkward girl with the big glasses grew, glasses got smaller, frame still slim, but it curved a bit, she had a tribe, a combination of cousins and homies who saw beauty in her ways, even when she couldn't see past herself, and got lost in her thoughts. She was trying to figure out how, how to make everything she saw when she stared off into space, come true. There were people around who told her she could, there were people who said she couldn't. None of them told her how... either way.

See, we get this life; those blueprints, we don't always know how to read them though. It's like a video game, and you're trying your best to beat this level, and get to the next. There are all kinds of surprises and monsters popping out to prevent that. This used to frustrate me so bad. They gave us rules; but, that guidance for the adult side of life was minimal. What they do give us, is basic. Most of us, just have to figure out most of what comes after that ourselves.

Like everyone else, I did my best.

She grew into a young teen, almost an adult, but not there just yet. I say that because as I look at it all, 18 is a lot of things, but it's not grown. There's so much we still don't know. Some of us sit there a while, cause we're still having fun and figuring it out. Time waits for no one though. Others, we have to make some kind of decision, and quickly. I had to figure out what I could do, to ensure I'd get out of an environment that wasn't conducive to my dreams. I had to figure out how to do this, in the best possible way. I got accepted to college, but I had no funds for that or clarity on how to attain the funds I needed. I had been writing since I was 6 years old, but I knew I needed money coming in, to survive while doing that. I had been working since I was 15, and hustling since around the same time, so I knew the difference between a job (legal and illegal) and a career. I had to figure it out.

That little girl on the porch, she wanted to be a mermaid, a writer, a firefighter and a soldier. She didn't realize that she was already a writer, and that would never change. The mermaid, well, that was years before there was a brown Disney princess, so we scratched that idea at the time. That left being a firefighter or a soldier. I looked into both. I took both tests. It came down to two things.... Which paid the best, and what would keep me off that porch.

Five days after I graduated high school, I kissed NaNa goodbye. Told everything and everyone I loved, that I had to do this, whether they believed in it, in me, or not. See, I had signed those papers at 17, junior year, and prepared for this. This was my way out. I honestly thought that I was gonna go, set a foundation in life, to fund the rest. I guess in a way, I did. It costed me some things along the way, but I did what I could, what I knew.

I left, I was now a soldier, in the US ARMY.

5'2, 99lbs.

 I was you....

I feel like it's a thing that some take lightly, yet it's heavy....

We should tell our children to use their voice, respectfully, yes....

But they need to know to scream when necessary....

We need to make sure that they know that No, is just as important as Yes....

They need to know that what's yours, is yours...

Mentally, spiritually, and physically....

It's yours...

Protect it...

Protect you...

Even when no one else will...

Your power, it's yours.

Power.

The word itself is strong. The meaning behind it, heavy. We all have it; some of us exude it without even trying, others try and force it, while some sadly hide it. No matter the case, we all have it, whether we realize it or not. It's in us, it's on us and it can be a gift and a curse. Power... that word, that thing, it's necessary. I didn't always know that....

I got off that porch...

I did some things most couldn't....

I was shown just how strong I was....

I learned who I was, and what I was capable of....

I was small in stature, but my heart though, it was bigger than me. That city I came from, and any adversity that I faced, those things I'd been through, they had helped me in ways that I didn't yet understand. I made it through Basic Training and everything that came with it. That South Carolina heat in the dead of summer was no joke. I did it though. That's one of the earliest times I can remember knowing that failure wasn't an option for me. See no matter what was in my way, I had to get around it. That mindset, that ambition, that need to be everything that I set out to be, it would pay off, but hurt at times along the way.

I got to my next training, which was for my designated job in the military, in Virginia, and life was, well, new. I had a little more freedom, but still a lot to do. I knew that once I finished that, that things would get even realer. I learned a lot there, picked up some skills and a career that would carry me through the rest of my life in one facet or another. I made a lifelong friend and I realized I was fine (attractive), to both the male and female standard. I learned that, that alone, in combination with the inner makings of me, could also make some people want to hurt me. I didn't know that some people would use their power to hurt you. I learned that hard lesson there, early in my career. He should've never been alone with me, or asked me to do anything other than my job.

In a moment when most would've lost their power, I found mine. I knew in that moment, that there were some things that I wasn't willing to do to win. I didn't care if that meant being treated like a failure. I wasn't going to let him or anyone take my power or tarnish my name. I'd rather be a loser who didn't give her power, who fought, than one who did. I'll never forget his smell; I'll never forget his face, as he told me I'd never make it in the Army with my attitude, and that I wasn't that pretty anyway. His face had an uncanny resemblance to a pig, so that was more of a joke than a jab than he realized. He promised to ruin me, and he almost did, but about that power, within me, I wasn't going to let that happen.

I knew inside that there was someone who couldn't fight like I was able to. I knew that just like the system failed me, it failed them too. I knew my little fight; to get out of there, to not let that mess of a man, or any of his cohorts who were in cahoots, ruin me or my career. I continued to lace my boots up, held my head high and worked my hardest through it all. I'm thankful to each of my Battles, which is what we called our co-workers in the Army; I'm thankful for each of them that protected me in those moments, the ones that noticed the little things. Male and Female; they protected me, silently, loudly, in whatever way they could.

It was a few people, who made more of a difference than they'll ever know.

In spite of it all, I completed my training, and still held on to my power, even if it was by a thread. I didn't let him have it. Some will ask, did I tell someone? Yes. Did it change anything? No. All it did was make my life harder. It created more obstacles, whether it was forcing me to change jobs all together, taking any free time that I had or reminding me how little he thought of me whenever he was unfortunately in my presence; it made everything worse. I would do it all again though, because I showed him just how powerless he really was.

Behind that rank, was a man who didn't get what he thought he should. I tarnished his sense of entitlement, and his jaded sense of being able to "make or break" a person. He scowled at me the day I was set to leave, and I smiled.

My power, it was MINE.

I was going to protect it, at all costs....

I was going to make sure I made it....

I didn't quite understand, but I knew that this was all bigger than me....

I knew one day that I would tell my story, on one level or another. I knew that somewhere, there was someone, who would need to know that they can get through this. I knew that my pain would help someone else heal. I knew that my words would start a necessary conversation for someone else. I knew that I would be able to say that I survived. I survived someone trying to break me, because I wouldn't let them use me, for their expense.

You are so much bigger than whatever has happened to you in this life. Someone else's sick actions, don't define you. You made it for a reason. No matter what, no matter for how long, your power is still yours. Never let anyone or anything, make you feel any different. You have everything that you need within you, even in your darkest moments. I shared one of mine, to show you that there's still more to you, more to life. Keep going beautiful, don't stop handsome... you've got this.

I made it out of that space...

 I made it out of that place...

I didn't let him make me his little cum rag...

I didn't need his cosign for success....

I walked out of there head high....

I felt like after that, I could do anything....

I was about to see just what I could do....

After I completed training, I had orders to report to Fort Campbell, Ky, THE 101st Airborne Division (Air Assault). It was one of the big ones, we'd heard stories about it, we called cadence about it. We were taught that it was one of those patches that's respected, that combat patch; if you get one, with them, everyone knew what it was. Well, I was about to earn one of my own. They were about to show me what I was really made of, I was about to do something bigger than me....

18 years old...

110 lbs.....

Petite brown girl....

On my way to this place....

Only to go to another....

I had no idea that I was about to make history...

There were going to be times that I wanted nothing
more than to sit on NaNa's porch...

I'd soon learn what it meant to have patience, as I'd
have no other choice.

Patience.

We used to count our days while in training. If we had 30 days, we'd say "30 days and a wake up..." meaning that'd be our last day there, that last wake up there, then we were out. It was a little thing that helped motivate us, remind us that whatever we were dealing with wouldn't last forever. No one prepared me for a time and space when you wouldn't know when your wake up was, or if you'd wake up at all.

See, I went to Iraq during a very raw and volatile time. I was there during what the Army called OIF 1, the first round of troops on the ground, in what would be a campaign that we (US Army) were a part of for many years to come. While ya'll were in the States watching them bomb Baghdad, thinking it was scary, crazy to watch and that the war had just started.... I'd already been there over a month.

I didn't realize that I'd be a living part of history. I didn't realize that my children's children would learn about things that my unit did. I just wanted to wake up daily, I just wanted live. I wanted my Battles (coworkers) to live, but all of them wouldn't. I knew that regardless of my job, war was a possibility, and that I would be a part of it when it did. I don't think they'll ever be able to teach everything you'd need to be prepared to deal with war. It's one of those things that you won't understand until you've survived it.

Once you've faced the things that I did, during that time, seen the things that I wish I didn't still see when I close my eyes, the same things some of my other brothers and sisters in arms still see as well.... You've joined a club that some later wish they weren't a part of. It makes you understand why Green Berets call themselves "quiet professionals". I can only imagine the weight they carry, and never speak of, as they endure even more than I did. What I endured was heavy enough. Those of us that were in the thick of it, don't boast; we barely speak of it, unless we're in like company or something about our experience can help others.

I was forced to be patient, keep going and keep fighting, with no clear "wake up" date. A year later, I'd finally be allowed to "wake up". I remember feeling a feeling I never felt before. It was all so surreal. I again, felt like I was outside myself, watching someone else's story, but I wasn't. This was my real life. I thought everything would be ok now; regardless of what had happened, I was going home. I couldn't wait to step onto NaNa's porch again. I got off that plane and kissed the ground... I was home.

During my time in Iraq, I fought alongside some amazing people, some beautiful souls. We would've died for each other; some of us are still friends to this day. We could go years without talking, and it's still whatever, whenever, when we do. It's a bond I could never explain. That comradery was the best part of it all, and one of the reasons that I wouldn't change a thing. That was one of the few parts of me that still made sense after everything I'd been through.

I had no idea how different I was, and how one action, leads to another action, and another and another....

I was about to learn a very hard lesson....

It'd take some time....

But, I'd find, that no matter the reason why....

My actions were mine....

Everything that came from them was on me....

My actions, big or little, mattered.

Actions.

To say that I was a product of my previous environment, is an understatement. I was a functioning mess. I was able to do just enough to say I was adulting. I was medically retired from the Army due to injuries that I sustained in Iraq. That was a blow within itself, as I felt I wasn't done yet. I actually fought to stay in a bit longer, but eventually had to admit I was broken both physically and mentally. I looked normal to most, but fought through physical, mental and emotional pain almost daily. They awarded me monthly financial support, lifetime medical care, an important piece of paper and medals no one outside of that life even understood.

I was so lost; I didn't sleep, I'd forget to eat. Esthetically, I was beautiful, but if and when I looked in the mirror, I didn't see that. I wouldn't let many get close; my "friends" were just people I'd meet in public places to drink on those nights that I feared closing my eyes and seeing my nightmares. I feared those nightmares so much, that I'd rather go be in some loud place, surrounded by strangers. I wouldn't sleep for days at a time. It's weird because I hated people and crowds (still do), but I knew I didn't need to be alone with my thoughts. So, out I'd go out, with my prescribed pain killers in my system, and drink until my face and tongue were numb. Then I could deal, blend in with the crowd, just long enough to not have to face what haunted me.

Let me openly apologize to anyone who attempted to get close to me during that time. I was so unavailable, and thought because I gave a disclaimer at hello, making my lack of availability clear, that it was ok. They chose to deal with my shit, it was on them, right? No. My actions were still mine, but I didn't see that. I wasn't capable of healthy friendships and relationships. I didn't even love myself at that time. I stopped getting care, stopped caring, just existed. The military reevaluated me at one point and took away some of my monthly financial support because it looked like I'd healed to them since I wasn't attending as many appointments and there weren't as many hospitalizations. Truth is, I was worse, I needed help more than ever.

I would lose it all before I got it together. I didn't know how to say I wasn't ok. I wanted to sit on NaNa's porch so bad, but I couldn't let her see me like that. I ended up homeless, living out of my car, showering at the gym and a friend's house. I knew I couldn't continue living that way. I sat in my car, by the water late one night, and decided whether I'd end it all right there or acknowledge my actions, and analyze what needed to happen to end this fucked up situation that I was in. Since I'm writing this, you know that I chose to live, and fight some more.

21 years old....

Curves there....

Body grown....

Mind gone....

It wouldn't be easy at all, but I didn't quit. I did what I knew to do best, something I'd learned when I first stepped off of NaNa's porch; I hustled. I did some things that some would shame, some I won't speak about here, but I did what I had to do to save me. I will be transparent about one part. During this time, I worked by day, and danced by night. Yes, I'm a strip club veteran too. I did all of this while fighting for my sobriety. In 6 months, I was stable again. I had a place, furniture, all my necessities, plus money in the bank and in the shoe box (true to what made me). I stopped dancing, and moved forward from there.

I'm not going to say that I never fell again, because I did, several times, but I always got up, and kept going. I learned that the reaction mattered just as much as the action. I am thankful for everyone who was there for me at my worst, as much as they are at my best. I didn't see how in those moments, but I knew I'd accomplish my dreams. There were strangers who'd tip me, who would literally tell me, "you don't belong here, get out of here". Many would proceed to tip me big in hopes that it'd help me reach my goal, while I was dancing. I'd smile and get back to my hustle, because in that mindset, I knew they'd say anything; it was all a superficial exchange. I was out of that life, off the stage at least (I did some hosting a few years down the line in a club as a side hustle) in 4 months, but totally on my feet in 6. However, those words, and many others taught me something....

No matter what you're going through, your light is still yours, and the real ones will see it....

Through the tears....

Through the bullshit....

Your purpose doesn't change....

Don't ever think there's no hope left....

I'm living proof- that it gets better.

I have several college degrees, as well as a long list of personal and professional accomplishments....

I failed many times in life....

I've lost it all, and got it back 3x's over....

I'm not ashamed of shit that I've been through....

It's all a part of my story.

Don't ever let anyone or anything make you feel less than.

Only dwell where you're treated properly....

Only listen to the words that matter.

Words.

Let's talk about words...

See, There's one thing that I realize remained consistent through it all, words. We don't always realize just how they affect us. For better or worse, words matter. Let's start with our inner thoughts. People don't realize just how detrimental that voice inside of our head can be. I'm going to go ahead and say voices in my regard. They've learned to talk one at a time, and don't argue much anymore, but each one serves a purpose. I'll explain a few ....

There's my conscious, little Miss Right from Wrong. She tries to make sure I'm on the straight and narrow, but my thought process, the other voices, and outside noise make her job hard at times. There's the unnamed voice who's just always ready, for whatever, whenever, and never fails to tell me fuck this or fuck them. That voice has become more stable with maturity, age and care for my mental health over the years. Then there's the voice whose words are never my own. That voice is a culmination of things others have said, both good and bad.

That last voice brings us to another point; the words of others matter too. I don't care who or what you are, how strong you may be, how much you say that you don't care, words matter. Words can make or break you. Unfortunately, some of the worst people in this life know the power of words and will use them to hurt you. You have to protect your mind, body and spirit in that regard. You have to learn to control what you can. Whether you realize it or not, words can stick with you forever.

There are times in life when we can't control our environment, but when you can, do it. Do not allow anyone in your space that is not conducive to your greater good. Now, don't confuse this with having people around who just affirm and pacify your bullshit, because that's no good for you either. You need people around who will speak life over and to you. You need people around who can see you, even when you don't see yourself. You need people who can say 'I believe in you', even when you don't know how. See, those are the people's word that you want playing back in your head from that third voice that we previously discussed. You don't need a bunch of people, just a few choice ones that are worth holding close.

I have been blessed to have some amazing people in my life along the way, even when I couldn't hear them over the noise. I owe them more than they'll ever know. I can say it a thousand times, but thank you. Their words helped me drown out every word the naysayers, and negative people tried to infuse. Their words helped me learn to talk to myself. In the midst of all of this, I learned that the most important words of all, were my own.

How we speak to ourselves, in every moment, matters. From your thoughts of you, to how you speak of yourself is so important. You have to be conscious and careful in your own regard. You define yourself; you affirm what you will and won't accomplish and attain. You need to speak to, and about yourself with as much love and adoration as you do others, honestly, more. You also have to pay attention to the times when you're unable to, because those are the times when you need to step back, do a self-check, see what you need, and take care.

    Everything that you hear, read, see, is an influence on some level. Make sure most, if not all of it, is what you need it to be. Make sure that you surround yourself with what and who is conducive to who you are (the real you) and what you are trying to accomplish. Make sure that you truly believe in your words. Your words are powerful, so talk to yourself, and all that, that entails, nicely. If you need a basis for it all, let me be the first to tell you, that you can have anything in this life, all you have to do is go get it.

Here I am.

Well.... I've given ya'll a glimpse into parts of me, in an effort to inspire you, on some level. I want to be for someone, what I did not realize that I needed in some of lowest or most confusing times. When we're in those moments, we can't always see clearly. I want whoever is reading this to know that even in those moments, you are amazing, you can do anything and you matter.

No matter the circumstance...

No matter what you've done...

No matter the mistake made...

No matter how much it hurts...

No matter what they said...

No matter what....

You can come back from it.

You can accomplish your goals.

You can win.

I hope that my words, my thoughts, parts of my life, will play back in your mind when you need motivation, when you need a reminder, when you're not ok.

I hope that anyone that's reading this saw only the beauty in it all (my story), even when it was ugly. I hope that those that read this book, understand just how necessary these conversations are. I hope that this book inspires more people to have these conversations, out loud.

I hope that I've helped you, on one level or another.

Part I was more about helping you, than talking about me.

Now that you know the main character, I might tell you more about her later...

Part II.

Here I am.

Lady (MaMa) + Daddy	Charles (G.B.D.)
NaNa	DC
Granpi	Kyle
PawPaw	Jermaine
Chelle + Ninae	M. Samuels
Zaria + Ari	Cousin Besaw
My TT's (All of them)	Juanita
My Uncles	Amanda
My Cousins (Ya'll know)	Heather
Ericka	Catina
ToyToy	Landus (My Love)

Amari (My Reason Why)

I love you.

Thank you.

My table is now full, and your seat is forever yours.

I've got a few more stories to tell, but you had to know that you're a part of it all.